P9-CAG-756

3 1257 01920 8650

Let's Talk About Pets

HELP!

I HAVE A HERMIT CRAB

David and Patricia Armentrout

ROURKE PUBLISHING

www.rourkepublishing.com

www.rourkepublishing.com

Photo credits: Cover © Eric Isselée; Contents © stephenkirsh; Page 4 © Jose Carrillo; Page 5 © altug; Page 6 © Myroslav Orshak; Page 7 © demoded; Page 8 © WonderfulPixel; Page 9 © Lola Granola; Page 10 © Elena Elisseeva; Page 11 © Stuart Elflett; Page 12 © B.G. Smith; Page 13 © Mari Anuhea; Page 14 © Eric Isselée; Page 15 © ZooFari; Page 16 © WonderfulPixel; Page 17 © Nion; Page 18 © Juriah Mosin; Page 19 © Joel Blit; Page 20 © Charlene Turgeon; Page 21 © Nancy Nehring; Page 22 © Luis Castro

Editor: Jeanne Sturm

Cover and page design by Nicola Stratford, bdpublishing.com

Library of Congress Cataloging-in-Publication Data

Armentrout, David, 1962-
  Help! i have a hermit crab / David and Patricia Armentrout.
      p. cm. -- (Let's talk about pets)
  Includes bibliographical references and index.
  ISBN 978-1-61590-250-7 (hard cover) (alk. paper)
  ISBN 978-1-61590-490-7 (soft cover)
  1. Hermit crabs as pets--Juvenile literature. I. Armentrout, Patricia, 1960- II. Title.
  SF459.H47A76 2011
  639'.67--dc22
                            2010012385

Rourke Publishing
Printed in the United States of America, North Mankato, Minnesota
033010
033010LP

www.rourkepublishing.com - rourke@rourkepublishing.com
Post Office Box 643328 Vero Beach, Florida 32964

TABLE OF CONTENTS

CRABBY FRIENDS

There are hundreds of **species** of hermit crabs. Most of them are sea hermits. They live in water. The majority of pet hermits, however, live on land.

If you have land hermit crabs, have no fear! Help is here! It is easy to give your curious **crustaceans** a home.

Crabby Corner

The name hermit suggests these crabs live alone. Not true—wild hermit crabs live in groups of 100 or more. For this reason, consider getting at least two as pets.

When hermit crabs outgrow their current shells, they search for something bigger. Many times, hermit crabs move into a friend's old home!

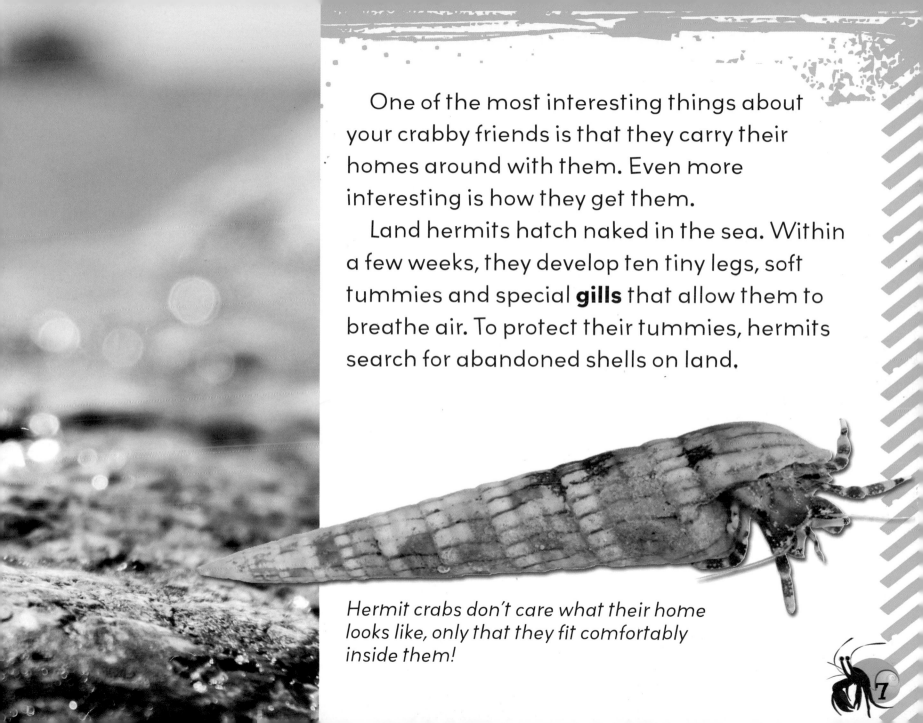

One of the most interesting things about your crabby friends is that they carry their homes around with them. Even more interesting is how they get them.

Land hermits hatch naked in the sea. Within a few weeks, they develop ten tiny legs, soft tummies and special **gills** that allow them to breathe air. To protect their tummies, hermits search for abandoned shells on land.

Hermit crabs don't care what their home looks like, only that they fit comfortably inside them!

CRABITAT

A pet hermit's home is its crabitat. Basic supplies include:

- Ten-gallon aquarium with lid to keep in moisture—a small air opening between the lid and tank is necessary.

- Sand and forest bedding made from coconut fiber—use several inches for the **substrate**.

- Non-metal food and water dishes. Its water dish should be shallow, so when a crab crawls in, it can climb out. Land hermits can drown in a water dish!

Remember, if you have land hermits, they breathe air, so don't fill the aquarium with water. Only marine hermits live in saltwater aquariums.

Other supplies for your hermit's crabitat include:

- **Humidity** gauge—humidity levels should be between 70 and 80 percent. This is very important. Hermits need moist air to live and breathe.

- Heater—hermits need warm air temperatures, at least 72 degrees Fahrenheit (22 degrees Celsius).

- Toys—driftwood, coral, and plastic plants.

- Shells—place different-sized empty shells in the tank, so as they grow, your hermits can move from one home to another.

Driftwood, coral, and plastic plants in the tank will keep your crabs interested and active.

HEALTHY HERMIT DIET

Hermit crabs are **omnivores.** They eat fruit, vegetables, and meat. You can buy them food from a pet store, but you don't have to. Feed them small pieces of carrot, apple, banana, and leafy greens. Cooked eggs and meats are okay sometimes.

Remove leftover fresh food from their dish each morning. Don't give them sugary snacks or junk food like potato chips. These foods are not part of a healthy hermit's diet.

Some crabs like peanut butter on a cracker!

Hermit crabs require calcium and **carotene** just like people do. Not enough carotene and your crab may fade in color after **molting**, from a nice reddish or orange color to a washed-out tan or gray. Brightly colored vegetables like corn and carrots contain carotene. Crushed **cuttlebone** in their food dish provides hermits with calcium.

Giving your hermits pieces of carrot provides nutrients that help keep them looking bright and colorful.

MOLTING

A hermit crab has a tough outer skin, or **exoskeleton**. Molting is the process of shedding the exoskeleton, so hermits can grow and develop.

exoskeleton

A hermit that is ready to molt might be inactive, dig into the substrate, or drink a lot of water. Move him to a separate molting tank with moist sand, for digging, and food and water dishes.

Just before molting, your hermit may seek protection and privacy by digging into the sand.

DID YOU KNOW? . . .

Hermits that lose an eye or leg will regrow them during a molt.

After a molt, your crab will look small, and his new exoskeleton will be soft. Don't be alarmed if you see your hermit eating his shedded skin. It is natural. His old exoskeleton has calcium and other nutrients that help his new skin harden.

Once your newly molted hermit is walking around and eating, he is ready to rejoin his friends in the crabitat.

Don't forget to place a few empty shells in your crabitat. A freshly molted hermit will need to choose a new home!

Most hermit crab experts agree painted shells do not make good homes. Paint can harm a crab if it accidentally ingests a broken piece of shell. It is better to offer several colorful, natural shells, so when a hermit is ready, it can choose a safe, new home.

Say NO to painted shells!

17

CRABBY BEHAVIOR

Hermits have their own personalities. Some like to stay inside their shells; others are active and do not mind being handled. When you pick up a hermit, hold him by the back of the shell, away from his large claw.

If his pincher gets a hold of you, don't panic. A hermit pinches because he gets alarmed or scared. Stay calm and quiet and he will let go. If you have time to get to a sink, place him under a gentle stream of warm water and he will release his grip.

Hermits have one large and one small claw on their front pair of legs. They use the small claw to eat with, and the large claw as a door for their shell home.

WHAT KIND DO YOU HAVE?

Most pet hermit crabs sold in the United States are Caribbean or Ecuadorian crabs. Caribbean crabs, known as purple pinchers, typically have tan heads, round eyes, dark brown or orange legs, and of course, one large purple claw.

Ecuadorian, or E-Crabs, will vary in color. Their eyes are oval. They prefer to live with other E-Crabs, so if you have one, get him a friend!

The large claw of a purple pincher often has a light-colored tip.

DID YOU KNOW? . . .

E-Crabs need to drink salt water. Pet stores sell the proper type of salt you can use to mix into their drinking water.

Pet hermit crabs can live for more than 30 years. If you find you can't care for your pets any longer, be sure to find them a good home rather than releasing them into the wild. They would not be able to survive without human help.

Likely, you will find that the longer you care for your hermits, the more hermits you will want to care for!

DID YOU KNOW? . . .

Hermit crabs are **nocturnal**—they are most active at night.

GLOSSARY

carotene (KAIR-uh-teen): colors found in plants and animals that convert to vitamin A

crustaceans (kruhs-TAY-shunz): sea creatures with outer skeletons

cuttlebone (KUT-uhl-bohn): the hard, brittle, calcium-rich inside shell of a cuttlefish

exoskeleton (eks-oh-SKEL-uht-uhn): hard, bony outside shell of an animal

gills (GILLZ): organs that absorb oxygen from water

humidity (hyoo-MID-et-ee): moisture in the air

molting (MOHLT-ing): process of shedding the exoskeleton

nocturnal (nok-TUR-nuhl): active at night

omnivores (OM-nuh-vorz): animals that eat plants and meat

species (SPEE-sheez): one certain kind of animal

substrate (SUB-strayt): the surface where animals live and grow

Index

Websites

www.hermitcrabs.org/

www.hermit-crabs.com/

www.pethermitcrab.com/

www.hermitcrabassociation.com

About the Authors

David and Patricia Armentrout live near Cincinnati, Ohio, with their two sons and dog, Max. After adopting Max in 2001, it didn't take long before he won over the hearts of family, friends, and neighbors! The Armentrouts have also had other pets over the years, including cats, birds, guinea pigs, snakes, fish, turtles, frogs, and hermit crabs.